VIGIL

Vigil

Notes from a Hospice Life

A.J. LAND

City Girl Poetry

CONTENTS

for all the those who have gone before.
for the families who have loved and lost
those dearest to them.
you are forever in my heart.

~ I ~

absolution

I rinse my feet.
The day hangs on, unyielding, glue and plaster.
I once heard absolution comes by water.
Where is my baptism?

Reality has become too harsh
upon my skin — leathered and callused,
heart brittle,
young bones already old.

I come to the dying, or they come to me.

Either way, I am not the person of yesterday.

Their knowledge is deeper than mine,
accessing truth I cannot.

Their eyes, pools of hard-fought wisdom.

Finished asking or needing like the rest of us,

they are actively,
peacefully,
contentedly,
resigned.

A tapestry laid out before them, examined,
square by square,
their lives are color-full and rich,
cocooning their hearts while bodies
slow to a crawl,
requesting, or demanding,
rest.

Your light begins to dim,
your skin starts to cool,

and those who love you cannot bear it.

I am silent, your hand in mine,
keeping space for all that cannot be said.

I sit your vigil
because you are real and true and here

because there is beauty even now
especially now

because I pray someday
someone will sit mine

because no one should die alone.

I watch you die
and have all your questions answered.
And I wonder, for the hundredth time,
what it's like to be you.

~ II ~

aftermath: a portrait of grief

A single second passes
sears itself into deepest memory
when irrevocable change
changes everything
about all the seconds to come.

They become minutes

that stretch into hours
that morph into days
that move into weeks
that roll into months
and overtake entire years
of a life
when the bottom has fallen out
gravity has grabbed your ankles
and deep inside the earth
it is only dark.

The tunnel is narrow and
dank
full of thin, stale air
and no
where you've been
is it lonelier.

It is a place you've always known
whether this voyage is your first
or fiftieth.

This journey
breeds
dismay and challenge,
for your body
knows
what is it is asking of you —
sweat beads on clammy skin,
shallow breaths elusive as reason
to the obdurate.

There is a way out but
the map is buried deep in the
recesses of thought and feeling,
archived files you
were praying you wouldn't
need again
in this lifetime.

At least not yet,
at least not now.

A wall damp with mold and rain
is the only thing holding
you vertical,
scaffolding weak bones,
reminding your brain
you are solid and true.

Your lungs function
just enough
to keep bearings
of body and space.

Time has passed –
how much, you couldn't say,
how much could it matter.

A soul-truth prevents complete collapse,
brought to mind by snatches of
clean air sneaking its way
down the line, brushing hope
against weary ears.

Just this comfort:
the sky has not abandoned you
completely.

It is faint,
the light-years between so vast you
can't fathom feeling it again
on your lifted face,
but the force that nourishes the
earth stays
its constant course,

cognizant of your need,
doling out measures equal,
one part energy,
another part resolve.

This becomes your buoy
and you make up your mind.

Mud caked into fingernails,
you claw and scrape at dirt and grime,
a hold found,
sheer grit activates
muscles and limbs, spirit and courage.

Gravity be damned.

You lie wheezing,
gulping oxygen.

You are splayed wide,
a starfish washed ashore.

The blue of the sky pierces your senses,
beauty so stark and forgotten
tears prick your eyes.

Now there is only recovery,
seconds and minutes and hours and days to
gather strength,
secure footing,
and journey through
the mountains and valleys
healing demands.

That first moment, from so long ago, is disappeared,
into the void that holds all the past in its arms.

Forgotten it,
the world has.

Though unsurprising,
it's a maddening ease with which
all else seems to move on,
with barely a backward glance.

That second has formed you,
a crucible of will and hope.

You are remade, with
thicker skin, refined and sturdy,
strong enough to
rediscover your place
among those
who endure.

~ III ~

phantom pains

Your initiation was a firewalk,
hot coals searing tips of toes
up to the crown of your head.
   You are singed and scarred, the person
you once were
transformed into a version
you don't yet know.
   You've been branded,
marked by the authenticity of human
connection,
vision renewed to see across the gamut
of human experience.
   You enter a space hallowed,
reserved for those who
face suffering with bravery,
commitment overshadowing discomfort.
   You are lost and found,
filled and emptied,
over and again.

Every inch of you is required —
heart, soul, mind, grit.
You've learned to speak in the language of truth,
even when your heart is crumbling
to ash at your feet.

This is a work of intersections:
your vulnerabilities and mine,
my emotions and yours,
our mutual confronting of
real life and real death binding us
to one another by rope thick
as steel.

Stepping away from such work is an
amputation of sorts.

For, over time, you have grown new organs,
special adaptors for your heart that expand
emotional scope,
the width and depth and height needed
to hold others' pain inside your own.

Love always has room to grow, and must,
or atrophy will grab hold of the
corners of your soul, squeezing until
your warmth is gone, apathy taking its place.

No matter your journey, when it started or when it ends, this
work will
leave phantom pains across your chest,
in your belly, traveling down your spine.
Now you know the taste of pain and fear, of sorrow and hope.

It is a part of you, and will be,
for the rest of your days.

And for all that it cost, and gave, and meant, and required,
you will see the scars, feel the phantoms, cry the tears,

and smile into the quiet,
knowing it couldn't have been any other way.

~ IV ~

a glimpse

He spoke of a lake, broad and smooth,
himself skimming across the surface.
Impossibly,
weightless and free.
A serene voice called out,
asking if he was prepared
for the truest rest from
labor never ceasing.

He responded, *maybe not yet.*
There is someone I think I love back there.
She might mean so much to me —
I need to find out why
my heart beats louder when
her name crosses my lips.

The voice let him go.
He drifted back to the material.
Flesh, bone, pain, hope.

The vision imprinted itself
upon his soul.

Can this be?
Was it a dream?

Yet my
inner eye still
sees it clearly,
though I've slept
a thousand moons
since then.

I found my answer,
why love calls to us,
bear-hugs us until we
believe it tells us the truth.
It changes form but
never abandons us.

I've held onto this tiny glance
all these years since —
it, too, has held onto me.

I am ready now,
to find my repose across
a lake broad and smooth,
with a current still and
water blue as
a star-studded sky
at midnight's hour.

* * *

I used to pay home visits to a Korean War vet. He had no shortage of stories, but one he often repeated was about a time he almost died from the cold in an open field. He was rescued and had a long journey of recovery.
This piece is about what he saw as he slept.

~ V ~

the patient

The looks they give me,
bout drive a person crazy.

They've got droopy, puppy-dog eyes,
angsty lines pulling down the corners of their mouths,
sympathy tinging all their well-meaning words.

They pile in, friends and family,
nurses and helpers,
all hours of the day and night,
standing over my bedside,
convinced something needs to be managed,
that I need to be managed.

They fuss and fret, arranging blankets,
baking casseroles, wringing hands and
clucking tongues like a new mother hen.
They are maddeningly sincere,
creating in me equal parts love and contempt
for their never-ending attention.

I can't really blame them.

It's not their fault,
not really.

They just want to fix what cannot be mended.

Their own health makes them especially guilty;
they can't meet my eyes;
theirs focus on the lint on my shirt,
on organizing the bedside table.

They are trim and active
and feel badly about this;
they don't bring up their latest marathon
or success at the gym.

They are not so healthy themselves
and feel badly about this;
they recall their New Year's resolutions
and gym memberships not being used.

Mostly, they hate being reminded that death always comes.

But pity is never a good look.

It's full of hidden relief,
hand-wringing helplessness.
It only says,
at least today it's not me.

Understandable,
infuriating.

I turn away;
don't ask me questions I can never answer.

I can't clear your conscience while
mine is a bramble bush,
picking my way through
memories and regrets,
the what-ifs and should-haves.

Just let me be.

You find your peace,
and I'll find mine.

Only don't forget about me
when your time has come.

Remember my strength,
trust this process of the universe,
and resolve to find
a gracious ending
all your own.

Nursing Home Notes: Diet Coke & Nail Polish

their hair should be cut and styled, on the regular,
just the way they like.
and their beards should be trimmed and tidied, on the regular,
just the way they like.
  they should wear their favorite sweatshirt every
day if they want, and their room stocked
with Diet Coke or Ben & Jerry's, for when the
fancy strikes.
  they should not sit hours
waiting for a cup of water,
simply because they
have no means to ask for one.
  their clothes should fit well and be kept clean.
soft throws covering frail legs prone to a chill,
swollen feet propped up for comfort.
  keep my drawers dry and warm, dear God, if anything,
don't let me sit in my own excrement. my heart can't
handle this, nor can my skin. they are too fragile,
they will blister and break,
I'll never recover.

I'm mortified, but surely you know this.
give me this one dignity, I beg.
   I hate that I have to beg.
   most of all, don't treat me as a child.
   I have much I could teach you,
if only you would ask.
   maybe sit at my knee, with a mouth closed and
ears listening, and see who you are when you rise.
   I still need to give — otherwise, my
end has already come.
   it's only a matter of a few decades.
they were our teachers and principals, our doctors and bus
drivers.
they gave birth to us and a place to land while we were
stretching our wings.
they built our homes and machines, our schools and cars,
they planted vegetable gardens and dreams of bright days —
they saw America was growing, kept watering the seed.
   in a place where luxuries are lost to times past,
where identities are sacrificed upon the altars of
age, debility, indifference
by the many,
   in a space where persons with pulses
thumping and souls
speaking have been reduced to
bodies in need of tending,
faces with no features, hidden by deep creases
and days on repeat,
   where poorly trained staff provide
substandard care because
good enough
has transferred from

the grade book
to the life book, a tick
just north of total neglect,
    where poor vision and poorer hearing,
often conjoined with thinking fuzzy and shrouded,
justify apathetic (*in*)action,
by those paid a paltry sum to just
pretend they care, but for
a few hours before returning to
the outside world, the one they hardly
get to see, the one that has nearly
forgotten they were here
before any of us ever were.
    the walls are peeling,
asking for
a restoration of
respect your elders
and
honor the aging
    and maybe throw in a touch of that
Golden Rule now
and again.
    for tomorrow it will be your bottom
sore and flat from too much sitting,
confined to the mobile prison
that is a wheelchair,
staring at four pallid walls,
hard-pressed to bring to mind
whether anyone
still needs you.
    ruby red fingers
pastel pink toes

the sun's kiss
the caress of the summer breeze
a squeeze of the shoulder
a kind word and smile —
　　these we will give you
because you have our respect
because you deserve
to be seen and know
your life has made
all the difference
in the world.

~ VII ~

existence

My days are marked by loss. It manifests in a variety of shapes and sizes, colors, and hues. But the timbre of the notes holds steady, resonating true and real. Heartbreak, sorrow, perhaps despair. Perhaps relief and gratitude. Death elicits a veritable coming to terms. It's a peeling away of control and security, a loosening of grasp. Fingers pried up, wills being tested, a letting go demanded. Everything that was held so tightly shows itself to be impermanent however we might protest. All is fleeting, both the beautiful and the wrenching, and in this there is small relief.

Sometimes the losses feel especially devastating or especially peaceful. Often, there are lives in front of me that may appear, from the outside looking in with very mortal eyes, as failures, or a sad end to natural consequences. A heartbreaking final chapter, it seems. Organs ravaged by addiction and misuse. Years of neglect take a toll on a body and on a soul. Has your spirit atrophied as much as your physical form? We pray against such things.

I want to ask you questions. Did your enlightenment ever come? Did peace find you in the quiet spaces? I cannot truly see you, on this day of wrought endings and final breaths. I see but a shell, the husk that holds an entire life, now being held by those who will carry your story into tomorrow. The end tells nothing of the beginning and no matter the course a life took, it started with hope, and possibility, and all the world waiting. I can't see the contours of a life, the bends in the road, the countless decisions leading this way and that. That there was pain, without question. Sorrow and shame, of course. But just as assuredly, there was joy, love, and hope, in measures that carried you forward. There was a mother's fierce gaze upon her child, new love transforming her where she stood. There was the laughter and play of childhood, a protective shield from all that life would send your way. There was the optimism of what could be, of what shape life might take.

And all that transpired from your sunrise to your sunset layered upon itself to result in this moment, this day, this goodbye. You are dearly cherished and surrounded by loved ones; you are alone and forgotten by all but the divine and those present to bear witness. But you live. You lived. And in the grand scheme of the cosmos, this matters the most. Let us not dare walk away from one another unchanged. For this, your very existence, is the point itself.

~ VIII ~

broken compass:
a view of dementia

I'm in quicksand,
quick
quick
quickly
sinking
solid ground has given way,
crumbled, disappeared,
my feet touching the lava of earth's belly.

I've lost all bearings.
Up is down,
down is up,
my life is a fun house mirror.

Where is true north?
My compass shattered—
this island is breaking me.

I'm not angry.
Only terrified.

My mind has betrayed me,
now I'm betraying you.

A brain misfiring, rewiring,
proteins growing, tangling, confusing
centers of thought and judgment,
memory and reason, a spaghetti
of neurons,
a system trying to fail.

Am I your mother?
Am I your father?
Your sister or brother?
The spouse you held
all these years?

I cannot know
the comfort of truth
anymore.

I never meant for this to happen.
I could say I'm sorry a million times.
It will never be enough.

When I yell and slap your hand away,
when I volley curses that never
before crossed my lips,
when I throw my food instead of eat it,
when I forget how to
swallow or use the toilet,
when I've become the child
to my own child,

I'm as mortified, horrified,
bewildered as you.

When I test all your patience,
and you don't know if you have
anything left to give,
know I'm feeling the same,
I just don't know how to tell you.

When I look like a stranger to you—
when you look like a stranger to me—
we are in the middle of a cruel trick,
one with no escape for
grief-stricken bodies on the edge
of the cliff.

We are in a maze,
searching incessantly for
a redemption buried
as treasure, hidden too
well, one we simply don't
have the capacity
to find.

~ IX ~

letting go

it was simply easier to go
staying had become untenable
a cattle's yoke holding me in the
cruelest of tension

letting go arrived
the sweetest release

finally
an exhale

I didn't realize how long
I'd been holding my breath

I had nothing left to give

you understand, don't you

please hold no grudge

I was so weary
sleep was
all there was
left

let me rest
let me rest
let me rest

my body tried telling me
what it needed

my soul knew

I didn't mean to hurt you but
I just couldn't abide
here any longer

please forgive me

one day
you will understand

that your work here
has drawn to a close

that when a canopy of the
purest light
begins to envelop you

and never before have
you known such serenity

that all will be well
in the end

and you see for yourself
this last breath
is as natural and holy
as the first

ABOUT THE AUTHOR

A.J. Land is a poet and writer who is also privileged to be a mother, a spouse, and a social worker for the ill and dying. She is constantly amazed that she gets to love people for a living. She is a seeker of the good and beautiful; her hope is you can find a bit of the good, beautiful, or inspired through her words. She lives with her family in Kansas City, Missouri.